All About Me
Write & Read Books

By Alyse Sweeney

SCHOLASTIC
PROFESSIONAL BOOKS

New York • Toronto • London • Auckland • Sydney
Mexico City • New Delhi • Hong Kong

Cover design by Norma Ortiz
Cover and interior illustrations by Rusty Fletcher
Interior design by Victoria Worthington
ISBN: 0-439-10616-8
Copyright © 2000 by Alyse Sweeney
All rights reserved. Printed in the U.S.A.

Contents

Introduction

Watch your young writers blossom with *All About Me Write & Read Books*! Kids flourish as writers when given the opportunity to write about topics that they know and care about. These fifteen reproducible books guide children as they write about themselves and their immediate world. You'll find that the books are easily integrated into your curriculum with topics such as school, family, friends, favorite animals, holidays, weather, and more.

The fun-shaped book patterns make the writing process lively and appealing to kids. With guidance, children can cut out the patterns and assemble the books by themselves. They'll also enjoy personalizing their books by adding illustrations and coloring the covers. Once finished, the books make an easy and beautiful wall display inviting others to read all about your students!

All About Me Write & Read Books will engage beginning writers of all ability levels. The books can be used in a variety of ways, depending upon the literacy development of your students. Younger children can complete one page each day, binding the pages together at the end of the week. Younger children will also benefit from the picture icons to guide them in their reading. Children are invited to circle the pictures and text that apply to them: foods they like, games they play, places they've visited, and so forth. More advanced learners will be able to write in greater detail and work more independently as they complete their books.

Encourage children to share their *All About Me Write & Read Books* at home. Children will gain valuable reading practice as they read their books to family members and friends. When kids share their writing with others, they gain confidence as writers. And as they gain confidence, they'll be motivated to write more and more! The books also provide parents with an important opportunity to observe and support their child's literacy development. Plus, sending the books home is a great way to open up discussion between children and their families about what they are doing in school.

All About Me Write & Read Books are a fun and easy way to foster confidence in your early readers and writers. They also provide a wonderful window into learning about your students as they share their own thoughts and experiences. Enjoy!

How To Use This Book

ASSEMBLING THE BOOKS

To assemble the books, copy a set of pages for each student on standard 8 1/2- by 11-inch paper. Cut out the pages around the book's shape. Arrange the pages in order and punch holes in the marked places. Tie string through the holes to bind the book pages together. Model the process for students so that they can assemble the books on their own.

PRE-WRITING WARM-UP

Set the stage for writing by discussing the book's topic with the class. This pre-writing discussion will help students activate prior knowledge. After this initial introduction, it is helpful to "walk through" each book with students before they begin writing. Read the prompts on each page so that students understand what they will be writing about. You may wish to complete a sample book and share it with students before they begin writing.

TIME TO WRITE

Explain to children that, like journals, *All About Me Write & Read Books* are a place for children to write down their own experiences, feelings, and opinions. Let children know that these books will allow them to share aspects of themselves with their classmates, teacher, and families. Explain that they will be able to personalize the books with their own writing and illustrations. Have children decorate their book covers when they have finished writing.

SHARE THE JOURNAL

Children will experience many benefits when they read their books to classmates, families, and friends. By sharing their books, children will view themselves as writers. Children will also develop reading skills and build fluency when they read their journals to others. And because *All About Me Write & Read Books* capture the thoughts, experiences, and interests of the writer, they also provide a tremendous opportunity for students to get to know one another. Children will realize that there are things they share in common with others, and that there are things that make every individual unique.

FOLLOW-UP ACTIVITIES

After students complete and share their books, you and your students may wish to continue to explore the topic. On pages 6–8, you'll find suggestions and activities for extending each book topic further. These follow-up activities include suggestions for related reading, writing, drawing, role-playing, discussion, and more.

Follow-up Activities

A BOOK ABOUT ME

Invite children to personalize their book cover by drawing their face and adding yarn for hair. Tally up the responses that children gave for their favorite animals, games, foods, and places. Draw a bar graph on chart paper for each category. Invite children to color in a square to show which is their favorite in each category. Show students how to read the graph and ask them to determine the most popular item in each category.

MY FIRST WEEK OF SCHOOL

To encourage positive feelings and a sense of accomplishment after the first week of school, brainstorm a list of things your students have learned so far in your classroom. Be specific as you generate a list of what they have learned. Here are some suggestions:

- songs and games
- books and poems
- safety and class rules

MEET MY FAMILY

Read *Families Are Different* by Nina Pellegrini (Holiday House, 1991) for a discussion about families. Discuss ways that your students' families might differ. On chart paper, list the languages that are spoken in students' homes. Ask students to share words in each language.

MEET MY FRIEND, _____

This book provides a good opportunity to lead a discussion about how students think they should treat their friends, and how they like their friends to treat them. This is also a good opportunity to talk about ways to make new friends. Invite students to think of ways to make new friends and role-play situations in which they are meeting people for the first time.

IT'S HALLOWEEN!

Read *Harriet's Halloween Candy* by Nancy Carlson (Puffin, 1984). Harriet hoards her Halloween candy because she doesn't want to share with her baby brother, Walt. But she discovers that too much of a good thing is not always so "sweet." Ask students if they have had any similar experiences. What did they learn?

HAPPY THANKSGIVING!

Use the children's responses in their books to make a class list of what they are thankful for. What else can they add to the list? Invite students to illustrate their ideas on a mural entitled "We Are Thankful." Display children's Happy Thanksgiving! books around the mural as a frame.

WINTER HOLIDAYS

Encourage students to present information about the
holidays that they celebrate. Ask students to bring in
something that relates to the holiday they are going to
talk about. After students have shared information with
the class, invite them to make cards for each other that
reflect what they have learned about the various holidays.
Children can also make holiday cards for other friends
and their family members.

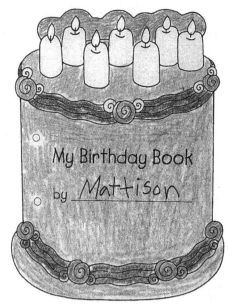

Teaching Tip: For children who celebrate more than one
winter holiday, make an extra copy of pages 33 and 34.
Encourage children to write and draw about all of the
holidays they celebrate.

MY BIRTHDAY BOOK

Make a birthday timeline by hanging labels for the twelve
months on a bulletin board or wall. Have children draw pictures of themselves and write their
name and birthday on their drawing. Ask children to take turns attaching their paper in the
correct spot on the birthday timeline. Keep the birthday timeline displayed for reference
throughout the year. When it is a child's birthday, attach a special birthday marker, such as a
cake or party hat, to his or her drawing.

TIME TO EAT!

Have children create a menu of their favorite foods. Bring in menus from restaurants as models
to show students. On chart paper, list the following categories: breakfast, snacks, lunch, dinner,
dessert, and beverages. Brainstorm food items for each category. Then give students one large
piece of construction paper each and ask them to fold it in half. On the front cover, have students
make up a restaurant name that incorporates their own name, such as Debbie's Diner. On the
inside, they can list foods they would like their restaurant to serve for each meal of the day.
Remind children to refer to the class list to help them with spelling, if necessary. Invite students
to decorate their menus with illustrations or with pictures cut from magazines and catalogs.

MY EYES

Have children think about other parts of their body in the same way they thought about their
eyes as they were writing. What are all the things they can do with their hands, feet, nose,
mouth, and so on? Give each student a large sheet of craft paper. Have students work in pairs to
trace each other on the paper. Invite students to write and draw on their outlines about things
they can do with their legs, arms, hands, feet, and so on.

MY FAVORITE ANIMAL

Lead a guessing game using the information about students' favorite animals on page 2 of their
books. Ask each student to share the information about the animal's features and size before the
class guesses what the animal is.

For another extension activity, invite children to research their favorite animal. On page 4 of their books, children write something that they would like to know about their favorite animal. Have children research the answer to their question. Provide appropriate books and resources.

OUR FIELD TRIP

This is a great book to do as a follow-up to a class field trip. Use students' books to compile a list of what the children learned on the field trip. Send the list home to parents.

Have students work in pairs to plan a field trip that they would like to take. Ask them to think about questions such as:

- *Where would you like to go?*
- *How would we get there?*
- *Who would we meet when we are there?*
- *What would we learn?*
- *What would we see?*
- *What sounds would we hear?*
- *What questions would you ask?*
- *What do you think you would learn on the field trip?*

WHAT'S THE WEATHER?

Make pairs of weather cards for a game of weather concentration. Write the words *sunny*, *rainy*, *windy*, *foggy*, *icy*, and *snowy* on index cards. Draw or glue pictures depicting the weather words onto the cards. Explain to students that they need to try to remember where the cards are in order to make matches.

For another extension activity, ask students to think about rainy day activities. As a class, brainstorm a list of activities that students like to do on rainy days. Ask students to share their responses from page 3 of their book about what they like to do when it rains. Encourage them to look around the classroom to think about what other fun indoor activities they can add to the list. Display the list when it rains for kids to refer to for productive indoor activities.

HOORAY FOR BOOKS!

Have children write a book review about the book they featured in their Write & Read book. Create book review forms with some or all of the following information: title, author, setting, favorite character, what the book was about, and why the student liked the book.

WHEN I GROW UP . . .

After students complete their books, have them work in pairs to interview each other about their future jobs. Ask students to imagine that they are grown up and that they are in the profession they wrote about on page 2 of their books. Have them think about what their day might be like as a grown-up in this job. Then invite students to "interview" each other. You may wish to brainstorm as a class a list of questions that children can ask each other about their jobs. To extend this activity, invite children to interview a family member about his or her profession. Children can share what they learned with their classmates the next day.

A Book About Me

by _____

My name is

_____.

I am _____ years old.

My favorite animal is a _____.

My favorite game is _____.

My favorite food is _____.

○ My favorite place is _____.

This is a picture of me.

○

1

These are some places I have visited.

(Circle the places that you have visited.)

zoo

library

park

beach

○ farm

mountains

I have also visited _____.

I would like to visit _____.

○ I would like to visit this place because _____

_____

_____

_____

_____.

2

I just learned how to

_____

_____

_____

_____ .

This is a picture of me doing what I just learned.

I want to learn how to _____

_____

_____ .

3

My First Week
of School

by _____

This year I am in _____.
(your grade)

My teacher's name is _____.

This is a picture of my teacher.

My teacher taught me how to _____

_____.

1

I met _____ new people during my first week of school.

Some of their names are _____

_____

_____

_____

_____ .

I like to meet new people because _____

_____

_____

_____

_____ .

2

These are the things that I like to do at school.

(Circle the things that you like to do at school.)

Read books.

Cook food.

Build with blocks.

Paint pictures.

Write stories.

Play sports.

At school I also like to _____

_____

_____

_____.

3

Meet My Family

by _____

(Draw a picture of your family here.)

There are _____ people in my family.

Their names are _____

_____

_____

_____ .

This is a picture of where my family lives.

The language my family speaks at home is

_____ .

1

All About Me Write & Read Books • Scholastic Professional Books •

These are things that my family does together.

(Circle the things your family does together.)

Play games.

Listen to music.

Go to the park.

Eat meals.

Read books.

Watch TV.

We also like to _____

_____

_____

_____ .

2

○ My favorite place at home is _____

_____ .

This is a picture of my favorite place at home.

I like this place because _____

_____

_____

_____ .

3

Meet My Friend,

_____

by _____

This is a picture of my friend.

I like my friend because _____

_____

_____

_____ .

1

All About Me Write & Read Books • Scholastic Professional Books

These are the things I like to do with my friend.

(Circle the things you like to do with your friend.)

Play board games.

Do puzzles.

Play sports.

Play computer games.

Play with dolls.

Build with blocks.

We also like to _____

_____

_____.

2

It's Halloween!

by _____

On Halloween I am going to dress up as a

_____.

○ This is a picture of me in my Halloween costume.

○

1

Last year I dressed up as a

_____.

This is what I might dress up as next year.

(Circle the costumes you might choose next year.)

animal

ghost

monster

superhero

witch or wizard

Or I might dress up as a _____

_____.

2

These are the things I like to do on Halloween.

◯ _____

_____

_____

_____

_____.

I like Halloween because _____

◯ _____

_____

_____

_____

_____.

3

Happy Thanksgiving!

by _____

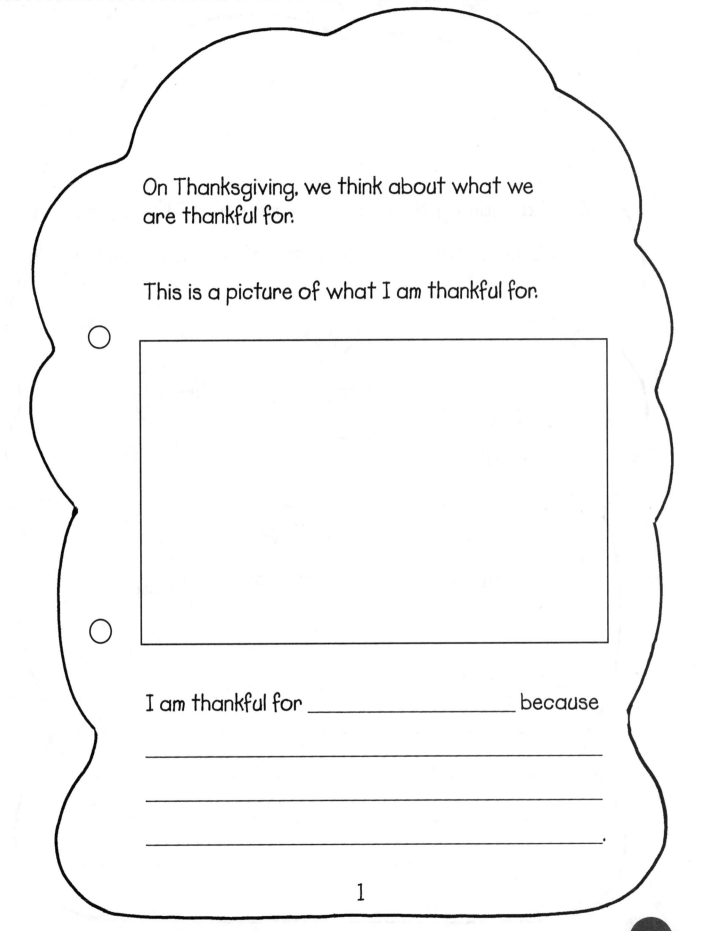

On Thanksgiving, we think about what we are thankful for.

This is a picture of what I am thankful for.

I am thankful for _____ because

_____

_____

_____ .

1

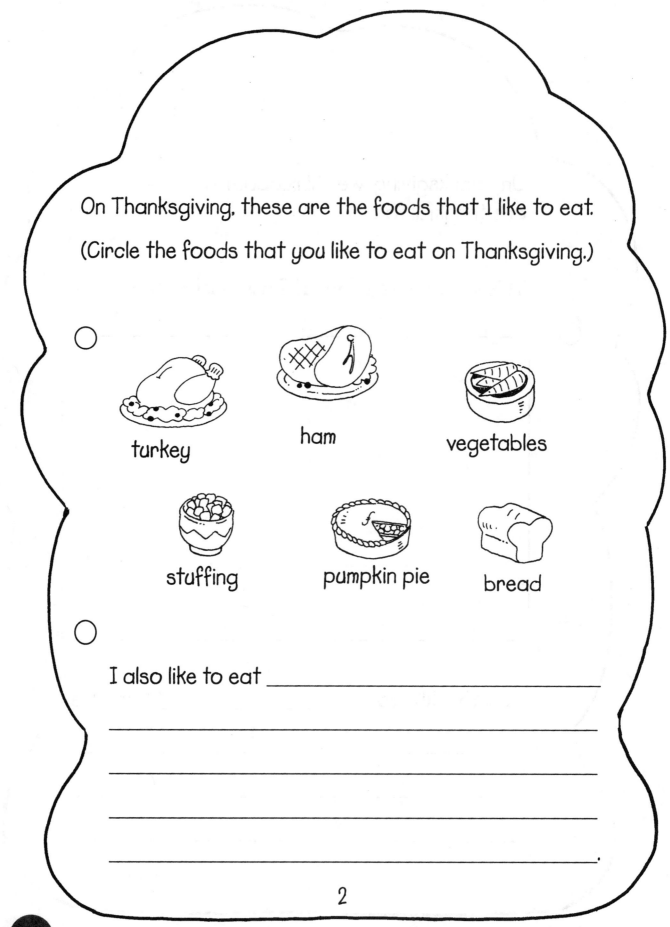

On Thanksgiving, these are the foods that I like to eat.

(Circle the foods that you like to eat on Thanksgiving.)

turkey

ham

vegetables

stuffing

pumpkin pie

bread

I also like to eat _____

_____

_____

_____

_____.

2

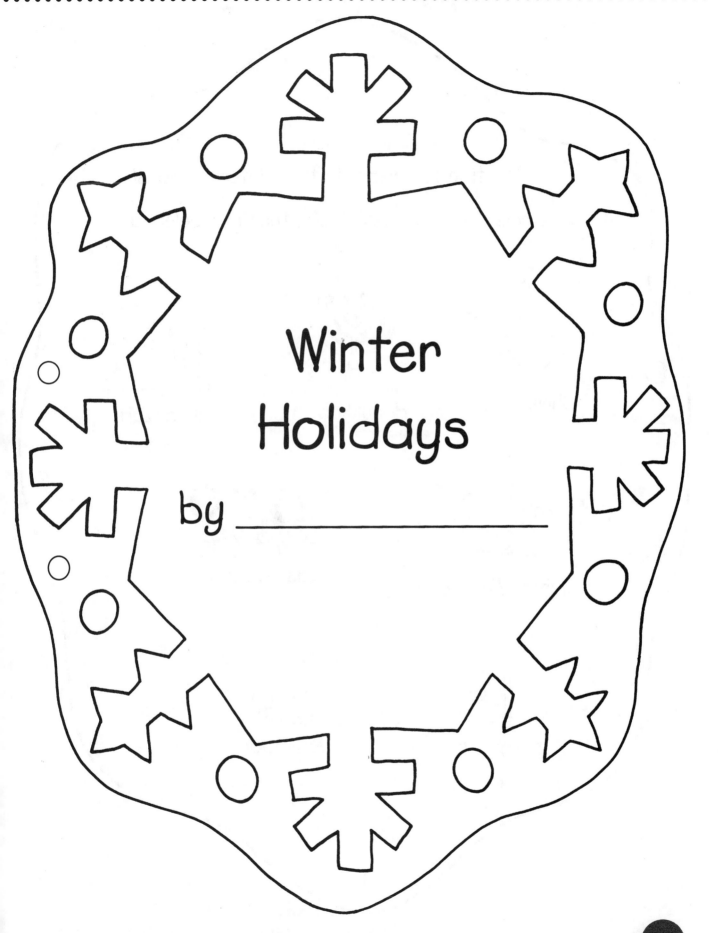

Winter
Holidays

by _____

It's time to celebrate the winter holidays!

(Circle the winter holiday(s) that you celebrate.)

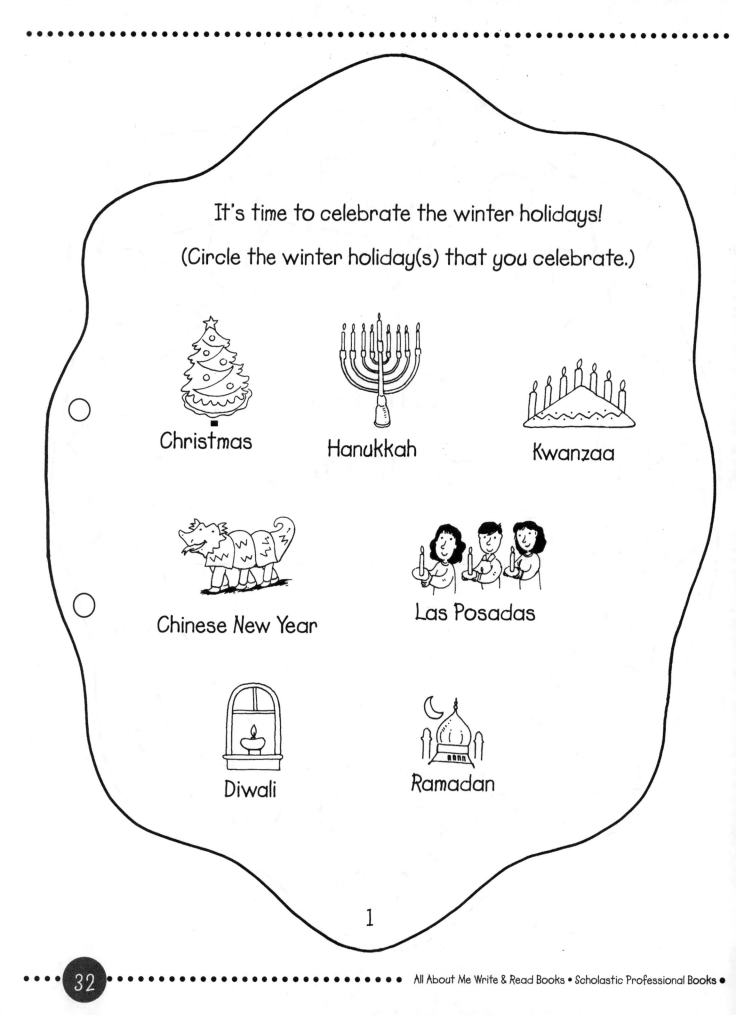

Christmas

Hanukkah

Kwanzaa

Chinese New Year

Las Posadas

Diwali

Ramadan

1

All About Me Write & Read Books • Scholastic Professional Books •

I celebrate this holiday with other people. Their names are

_____

_____ .

This is a picture of something special we do on this holiday.

In this picture I am _____

_____

_____ .

2

This is a picture of the food that I like to eat on this holiday.

My favorite things to eat during this holiday are

_____

_____ .

Holidays are special because _____

_____

_____ .

3

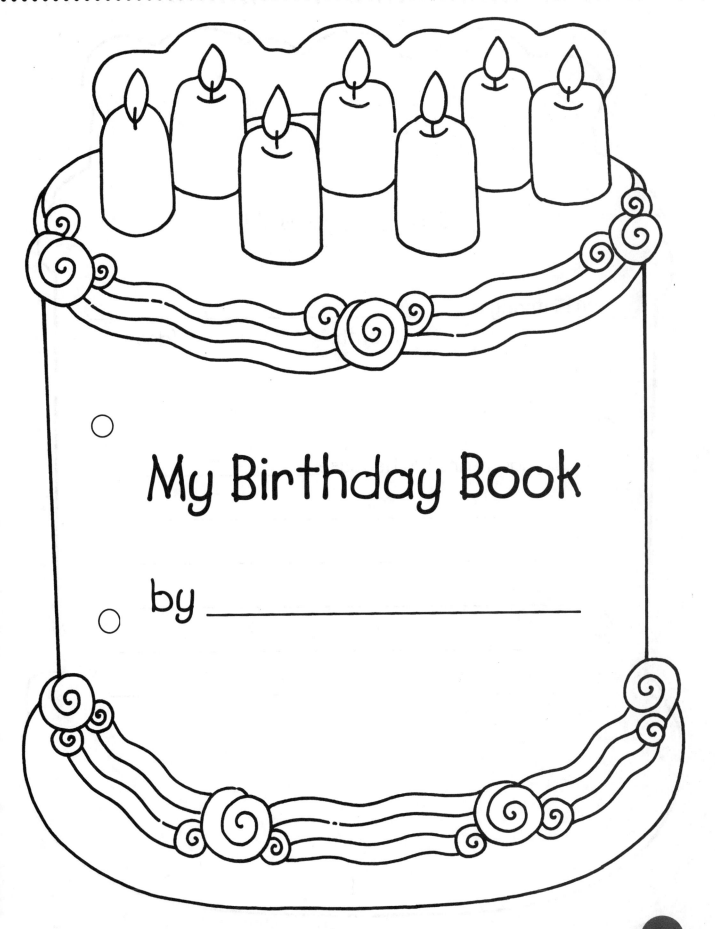

My Birthday Book

by _____

I am _____ years old.

My birthday is _____ _____.
(month) (day)

Birthdays are fun because _____

_____

_____

_____

_____

_____.

1

All About Me Write & Read Books • Scholastic Professional Books •

This is a picture of what I would like to do on *my* birthday.

On my birthday, I would like to _____

_____

_____.

I would like to celebrate my birthday with these

people: _____

_____.

2

This is a picture of what I would
like to eat on my birthday.

On my birthday, I would also like to eat _____

_____

_____

_____.

3

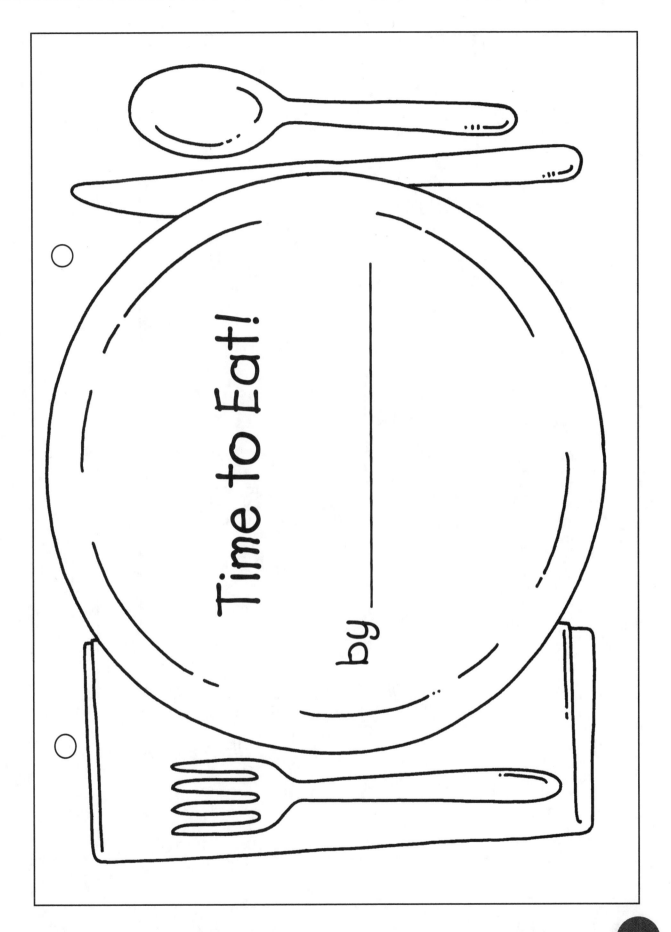

Time to Eat!

by _____

These are some foods that I like to eat.

(Circle what you like to eat.)

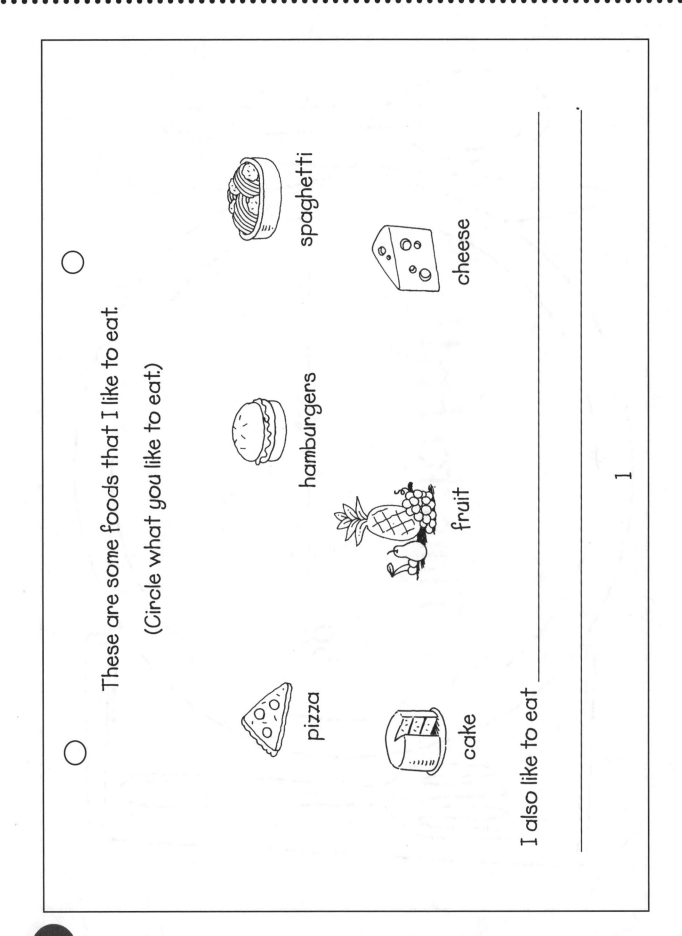

spaghetti

cheese

hamburgers

fruit

pizza

cake

I also like to eat _____

1

For breakfast, I like to eat _____.

For lunch, I like to eat_____.

2

For dinner, I like to eat _____.

Here is a picture of me enjoying my dessert!

3

All About Me Write & Read Books • Scholastic Professional Books •

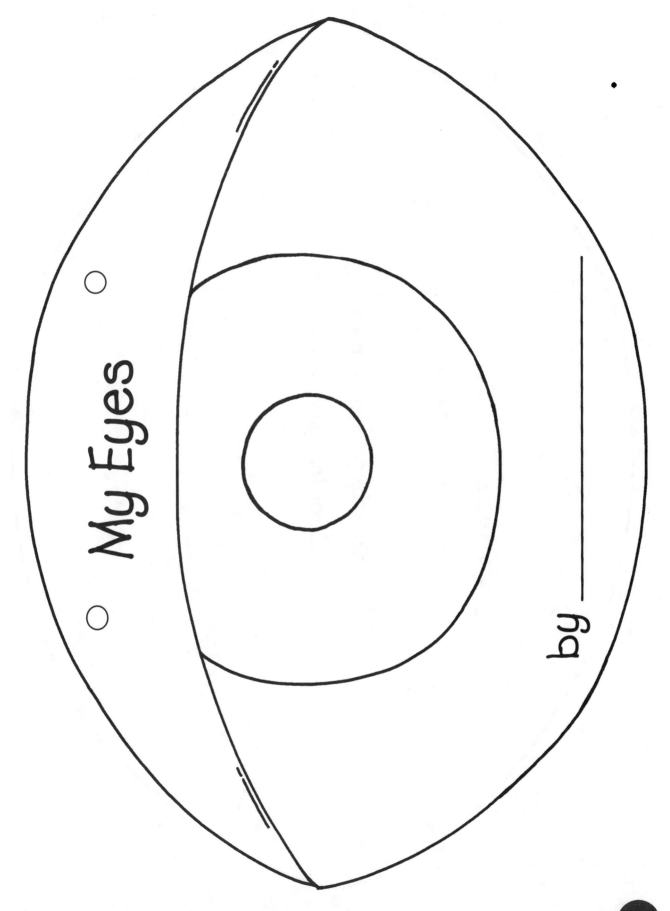

My Eyes

by _____

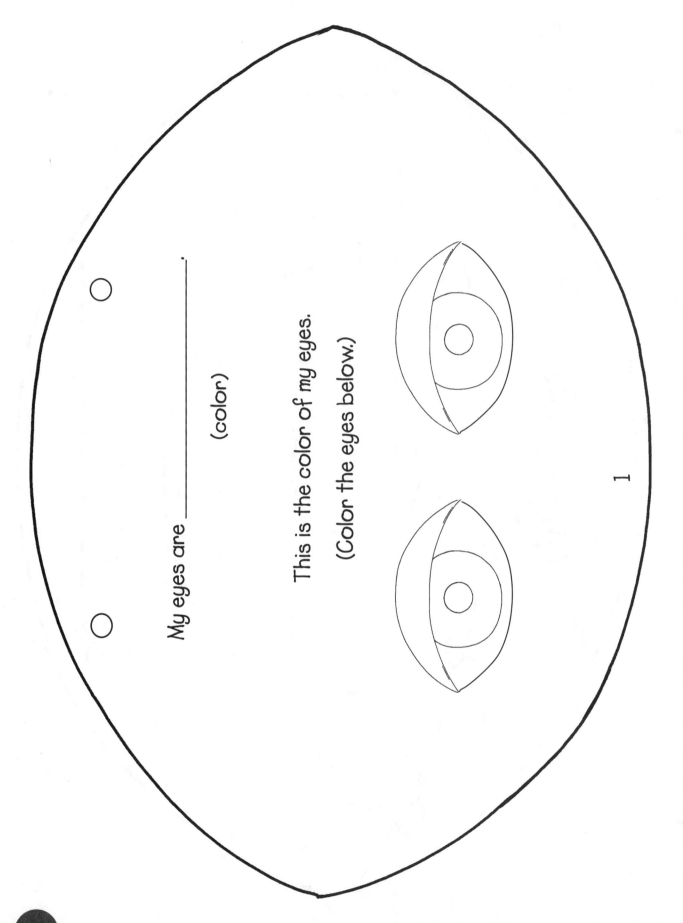

My eyes are _____
(color)

This is the color of my eyes.

(Color the eyes below.)

1

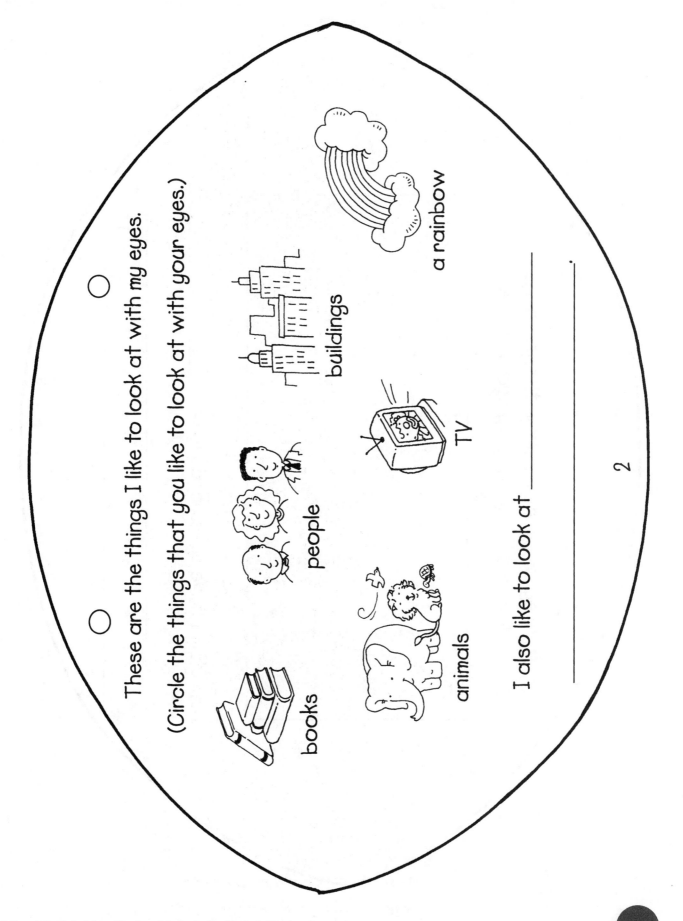

These are the things I like to look at with my eyes.

(Circle the things that you like to look at with your eyes.)

books

people

animals

buildings

TV

a rainbow

I also like to look at _____

2

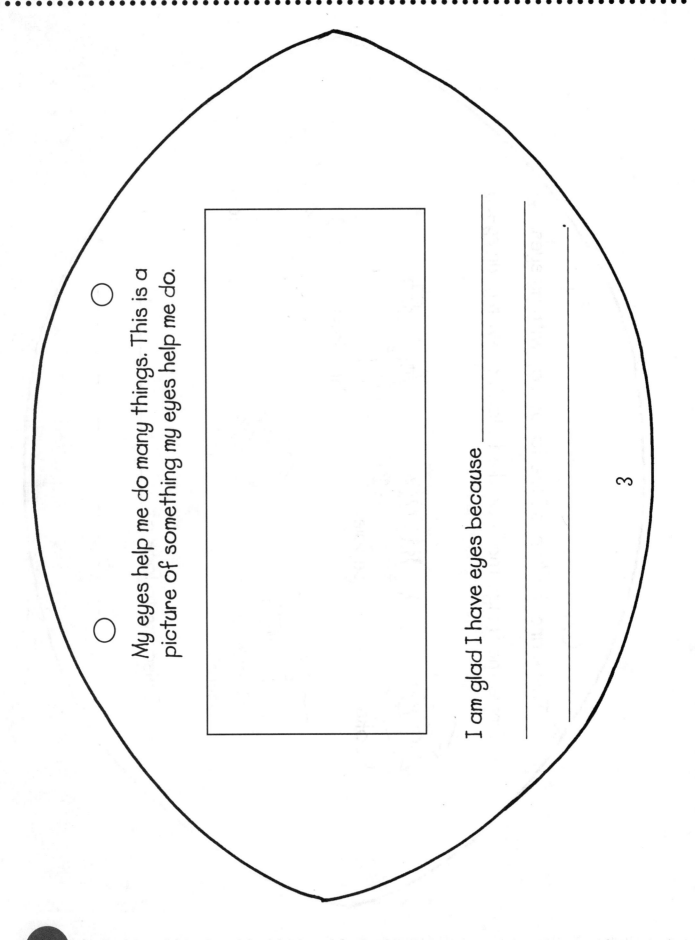

My eyes help me do many things. This is a picture of something my eyes help me do.

I am glad I have eyes because _____

3

My Favorite Animal

by _____

I like this animal because _____

_____

_____ .

This is a picture of my favorite animal.

1

My favorite animal has these things.

(Circle the things that your favorite animal has.)

fur

whiskers

feathers

fins

scales

claws

My favorite animal is bigger than a _____

_____,

but smaller than a _____

_____.

2

This is something that I know about my favorite animal:

_____

_____

_____.

○ This is something that I want to know about my favorite animal:

_____

_____

_____.

If I had my favorite animal as a pet, I would name it

○ _____.

3

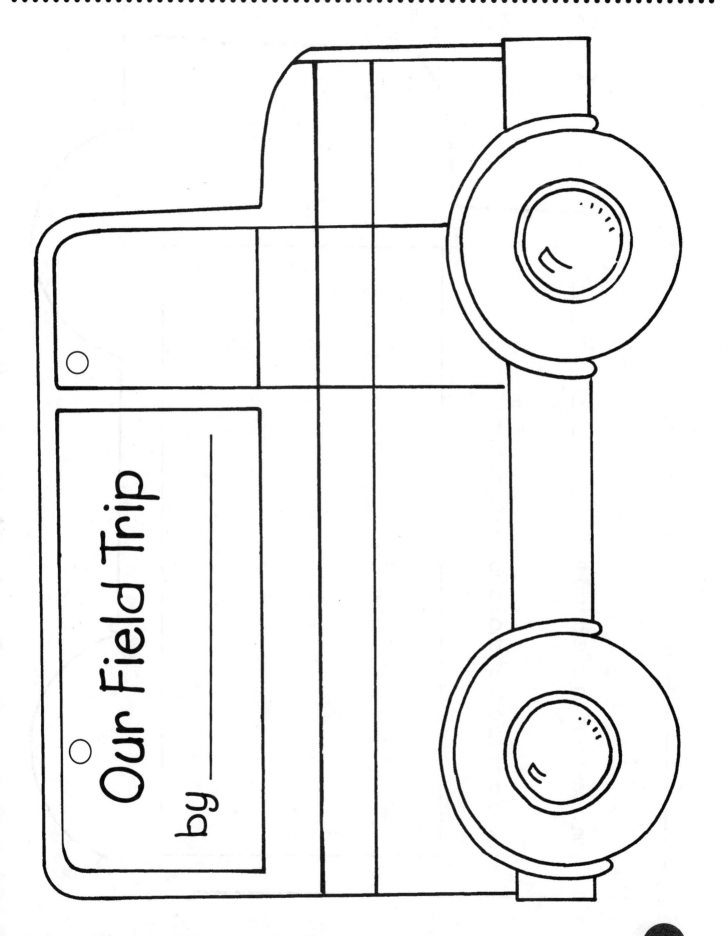

Our Field Trip

by _____

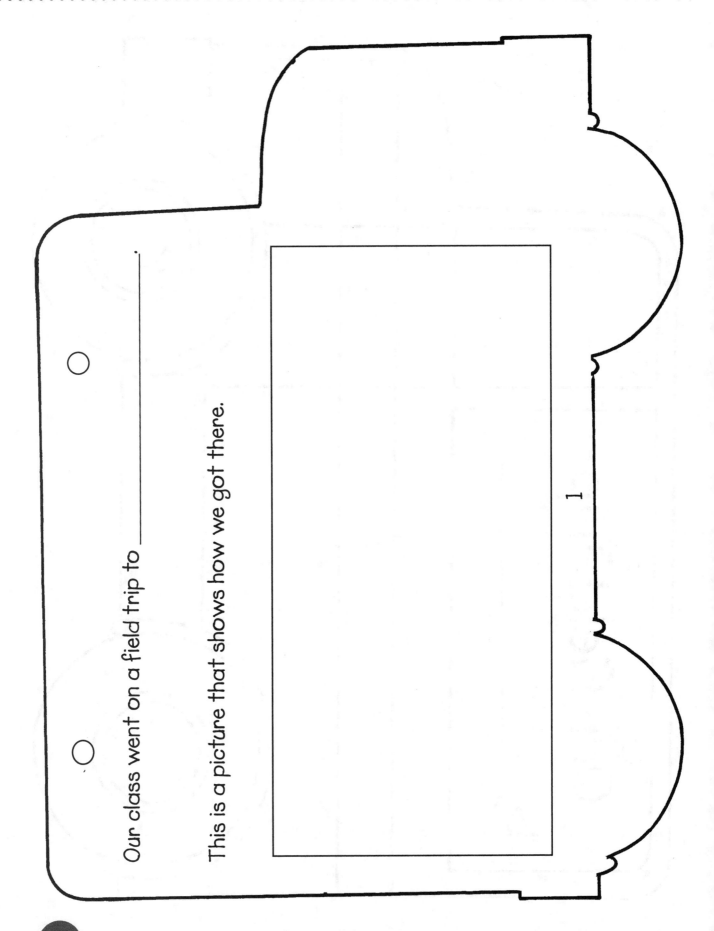

Our class went on a field trip to _____.

This is a picture that shows how we got there.

1

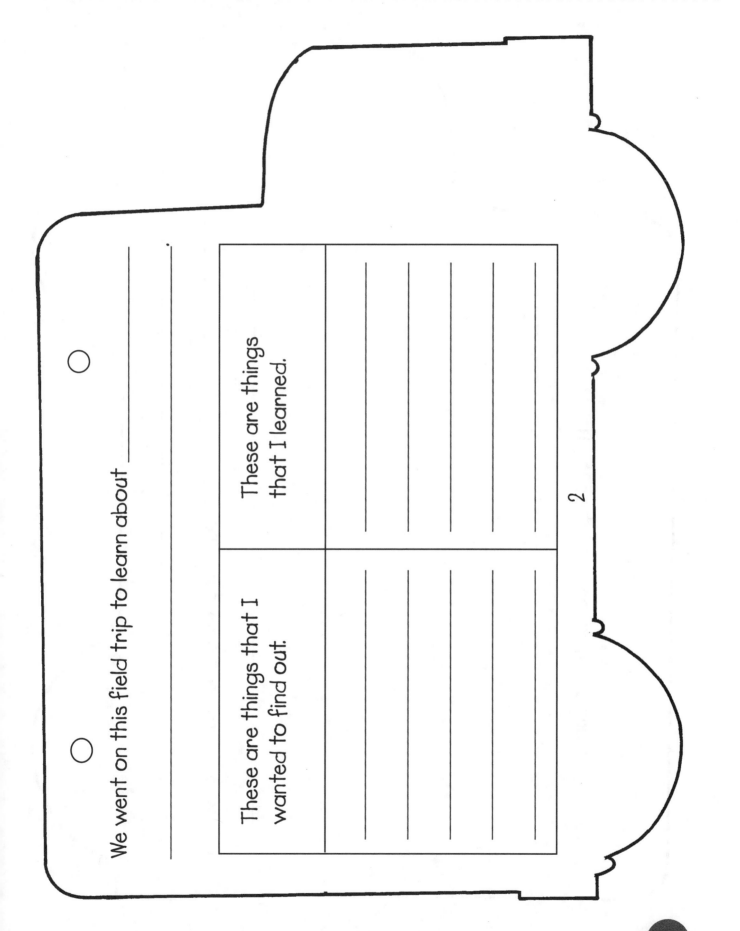

We went on this field trip to learn about

These are things that I wanted to find out:

These are things that I learned.

2

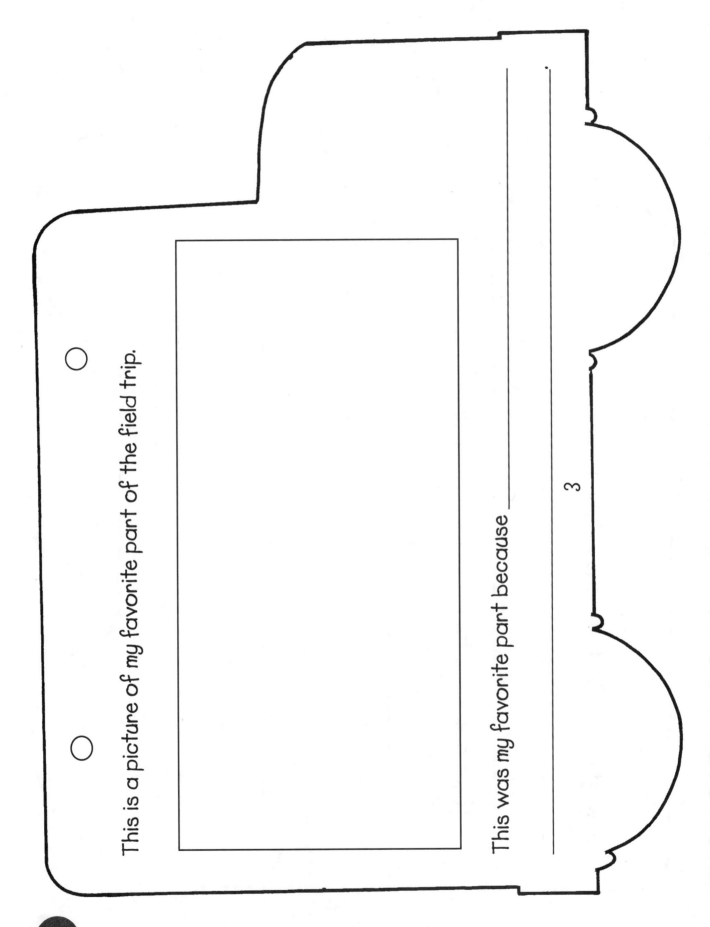

This is a picture of my favorite part of the field trip.

This was my favorite part because _____

3

What's the Weather?

by _____

When I look out the window today, the weather looks like this.

Today, the weather is _____

1

These are words that describe the weather where I live.

(Circle the words that describe what the weather can be like where you live.)

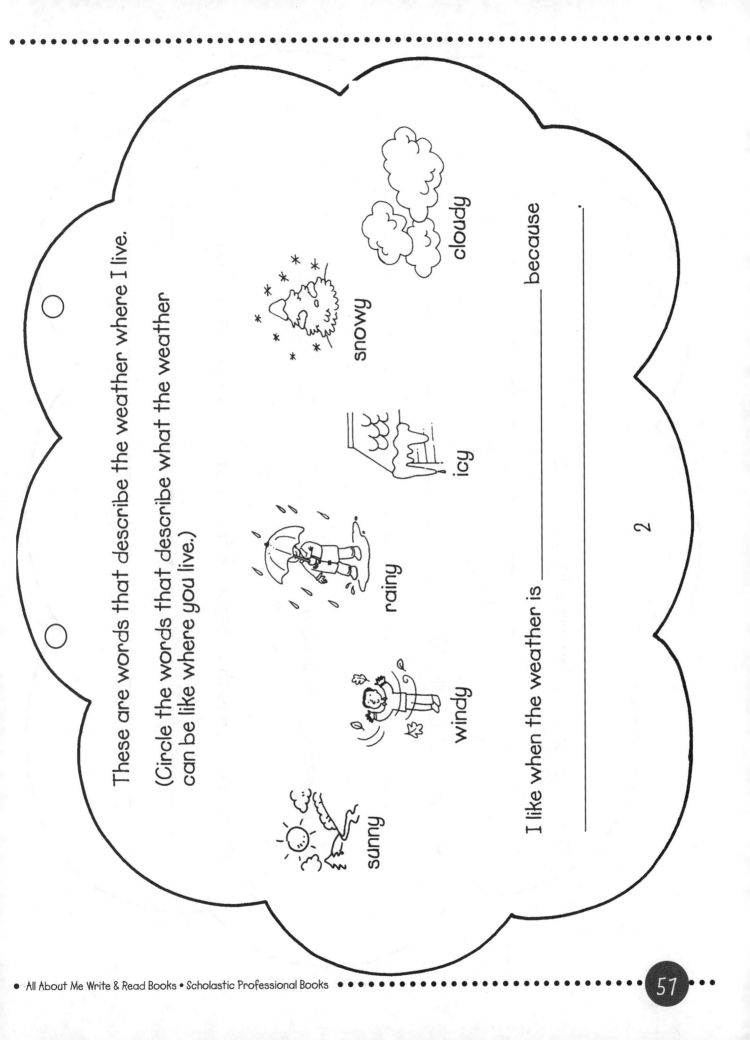

sunny

windy

rainy

icy

snowy

cloudy

I like when the weather is _____ because _____.

2

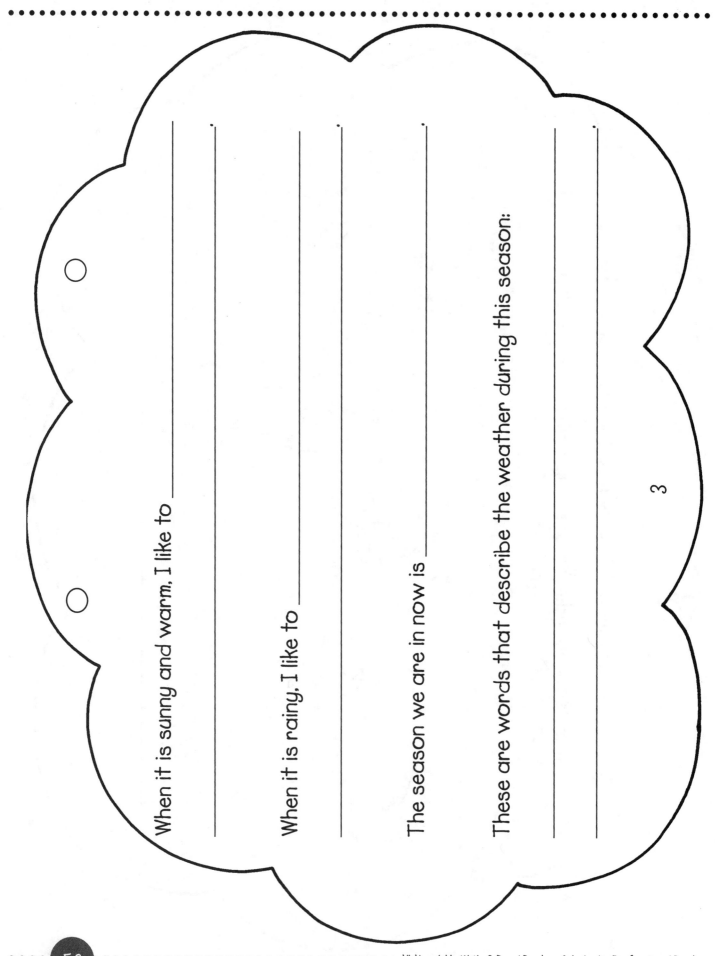

When it is sunny and warm, I like to _____

When it is rainy, I like to _____

The season we are in now is _____

These are words that describe the weather during this season: _____

3

Hooray for Books!

by

_____

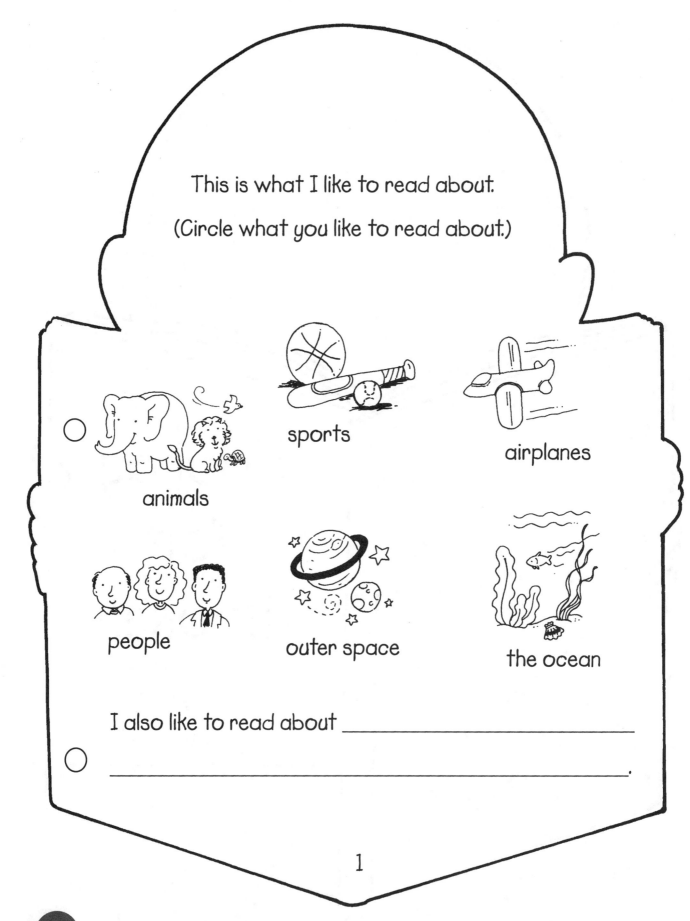

This is what I like to read about.

(Circle what you like to read about.)

sports

airplanes

animals

people

outer space

the ocean

I also like to read about _____

_____ .

1

One of my favorite books is _____

_____.

This is what the book's cover looks like.

This book is about _____

_____.

I like this book because _____

_____.

2

When I
Grow Up...

by _____

This is what I would like to be when I grow up.

(Circle one or more.)

teacher

doctor

police officer

artist

astronaut

athlete

Or I would like to be a _____

_____ when I grow up.

1

This is a picture of me as a

_____.

(What you would like to be when you grow up.)

I would like to be a _____

because _____

_____.

This is an important job because _____

_____

_____.

2